My EYES and ME Growing to Three

WRITTEN BY
Lisa M. Bennett O.D.

ILLUSTRATED BY
Damien Dugger

*For those who have been there from the beginning,
Mi Hermana and the crew from back in the day at store 061.*

Bennett, Lisa M. *My Eyes and Me Growing to Three*

All rights reserved. Copyright © 2022 by Lisa M. Bennett
Published by KWE Publishing
Cover and interior art by Damien Dugger
Cover layout and book design by Liona Design Co., www.lionadesignco.com

No part of this book may be reproduced in any form or by any electronic or mechanical means, including information storage and retrieval systems, without written permission from the publisher or author, except for the use of brief quotations in a book review.

ISBNs: 978-1-7369232-0-7 paperback 978-1-7369232-1-4 ebook
Library of Congress Control Number: 2021923354

You can contact Dr. Lisa M. Bennett at:
https://lisambennett.pubsitepro.com/ or at Frequencymediarva@gmail.com.

KWE Publishing LLC.
www.kwepub.com

Note to the Reader

Hello there,

One day in 2018, I saw a need. Riding with a team on a traveling optical van, I was prepared to offer free eye exams to children in a neighborhood in Richmond, Virginia. We were expecting dozens of moms to bring their children to have their precious eyesight checked. Only two moms brought their children to us. Initially, I was discouraged. And then, I saw an opportunity.

As an optometrist who has been providing primary care eye exams to all ages for more than 20 years, I have noticed that children often aren't seen often in optometry offices for routine exams, despite the statistic that one in four children have a problem seeing. Since 1996, I've made it my mission to increase the number of children receiving full eye exams—yes, the same eye exam that adults receive. I have written *My Eyes and Me Growing to Three* to inform caregivers—parents, teachers, health professionals and others—about the importance of vision for children's development.

The intention for *My Eyes and Me Growing to Three* is three-fold: to entertain, to educate, and to encourage action. The delightful illustrations of the main character, Mikey, by Damien Dugger will keep you engaged. The information shared in the text of this book is factual and I have strived to keep the information accurate about the development of the eye in children. Many readers who have read this book have remarked, "I didn't know that!" And the action I encourage you to take is to book an eye appointment for the children for whom you care before or shortly after their third birthday.

I've written this book for parents. The beautiful illustrations allow for it to be read to children as well. I personally consider it appropriate for young kids from 8 to about 12 years of age. Since this book illustrates and describes what happens to Mikey as he grows from conception to the age of three, take this into consideration as you share the book.

Thank you so much!
Author Lisa M Bennett, OD

Shhhh...Mommy does not know I am here yet.

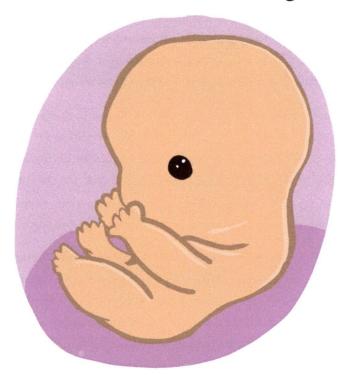

My name is Mikey! I am only **2 WEEKS** inside my mommy growing to be a baby BUT my eyes are already starting to grow.

They are funny — my eyes grow from my brain but they are on the side of my head — where my ears should be!

I have to start right away to develop my vision—it's going to help me learn so much.

I am this big...
about the size of a poppy seed.

So I am at **WEEK 6** of becoming a baby.

Mom is starting to suspect that I am here.

I am going to keep growing – now I am about .5 inches, about the size of a sweet pea.

My eyes are moving to the front of my face — it's a good thing because my ears are starting to grow now. I am going to start hearing Mommy's voice soon!

4"

It's going to take another 6 weeks for my eyes to get in their right place.
At **12 WEEKS,** I will be the size of a lime.

Between **6–12 WEEKS,** my eyes continue to develop while moving to the right place. I am going to keep my eyelids closed for a few months while I finish making my eyeballs.

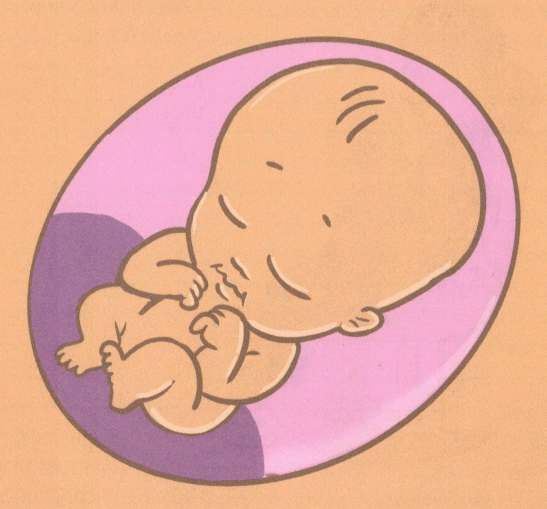

I am **25–35 WEEKS** inside mommy (6–9 months).

Everyone keeps telling mommy how big she is now.

At 6 months I am about the size of a cabbage.

I am putting the finishing touches
on everything, including my eyes.

My eye muscles are complete. They move
my eyes up and down and side to side.

I am going to practice opening and closing
my eyelids now.

I can hear my family. I can't wait to see my family!

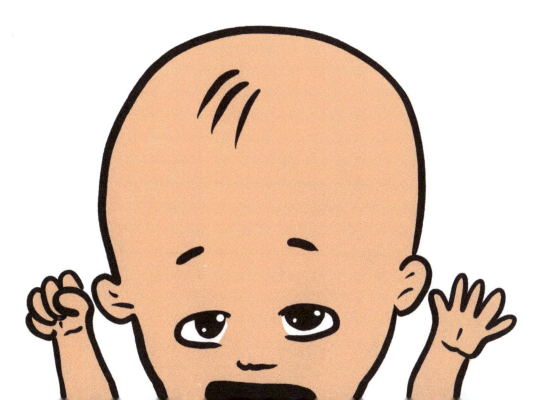

My cornea and lens are
complete. Those are the
parts that focus the light.

My retina is *almost* complete.
It is the seeing part and needs
light to finish developing.

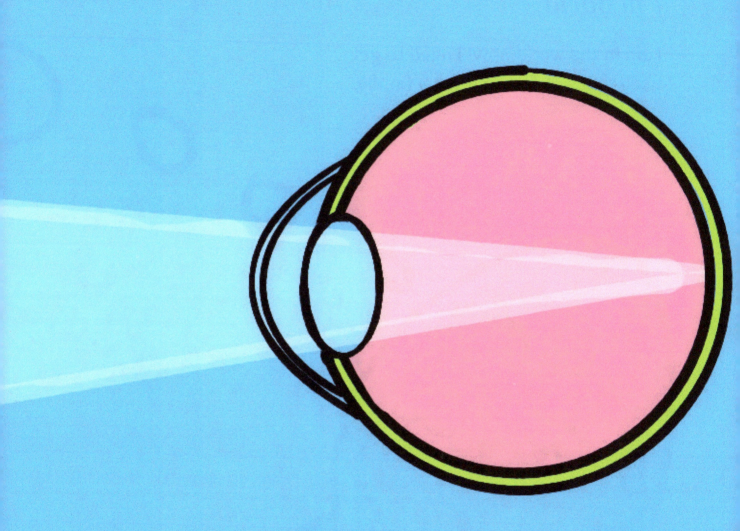

Now I need light! I need to get born!

I'm born!

I am in the world now! I need to get used to it and bond with my family.

This is how I see right after I am born because my retina is not completely ready, because it was dark in mommy's tummy.

My eyes do not know how to focus and they are not used to the light. That's why I am blinking a lot now. It is so bright out here in the world!

Mommy is always snuggling and kissing and feeding me and I am so glad because she is my whole world.

I know it is Mommy, I know her voice from before I was born. I can see about 8–10 inches. When she comes close, I see her, and I am happy. And I smile.

I am 0–3 months.

Things that are far away are not clear now but that is okay. Blurriness will actually help my retina learn to focus better, kind of like a camera lens.

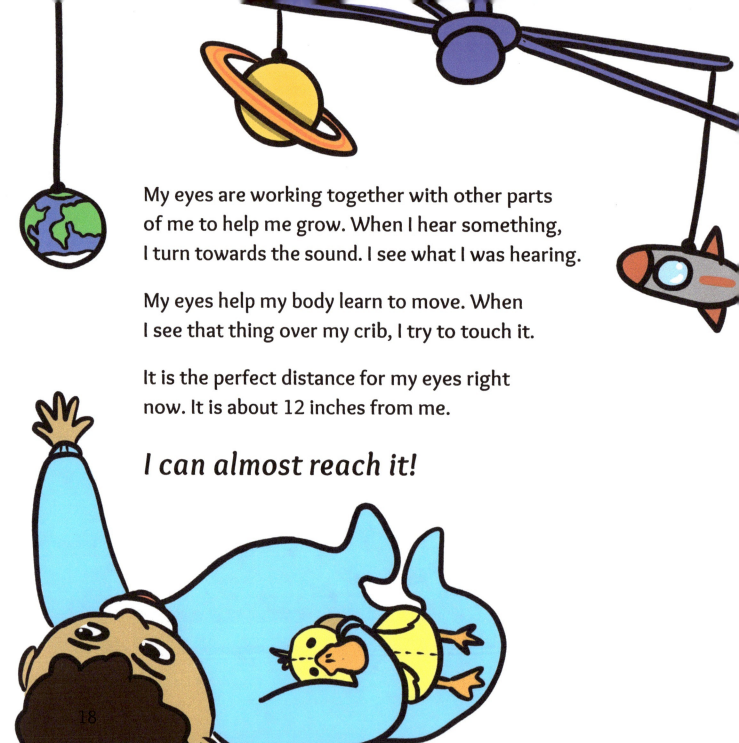

My eyes are working together with other parts of me to help me grow. When I hear something, I turn towards the sound. I see what I was hearing.

My eyes help my body learn to move. When I see that thing over my crib, I try to touch it.

It is the perfect distance for my eyes right now. It is about 12 inches from me.

I can almost reach it!

I am 4–8 months old.

I am learning my body.

When I lay on my back, I see my feet. I see my hands. I see my legs. I see my arms.

I need to get my neck strong so I can lift up my big head. Mommy puts me on my tummy so I will raise my head to see...at 6 months I can see all the way across the room.

I can hear people and I want to know what they are doing!

Pretty soon I am going to turn over so I can see better!

I am 9–18 months.

Oh boy, it's on now! I can move!

I have figured out that I have arms and legs on each side of me.

If I move one side and then the other, then I move! Then I will be closer to that toy that I see is across the room!

I can move a lot of different ways!

At first, I am moving on my bottom.

Soon enough I am going to stand up.
Look at all the stuff up here on the table!

Finally, I am going to walk. So cool!

I can also remember brother's face and know when he puts his mouth and eyes a certain way that means fun, fun fun!

I am 19–36 months. I have so much to do!

I have to walk.
I have to run.

I have to talk.

I have to play with other kids my age.

My eyes are going to help me so much!

I can do the big stuff like move my head and hand like him. But I can't quite move my mouth like him yet.

"Do it again, dad. I want to get this right!"

I'm three!

Wow! That was a lot of learning to get to three.

Now we have to check my eyes at the optometrist's office. This is a critical time for me. My brain will be making some major changes now.

We have to make sure my eyes stay healthy.

"It's OK, Mommy, I don't need to know my ABCs to have an eye exam. I can look at shapes! Just call 'em, the doctor knows what to do!"

I am so glad Mommy got my eyes checked.

The eye test was so easy and fun too! I just said the shapes and the eye doctor looked at my eyes with a lot of different lights.

My eyes are healthy!

My optometrist makes sure my eyes keep helping me.

It is time for me to go to preschool.

I can tell from the laughing that the other kids are having fun. I see them over there and I want to play with them and have fun too.

I see kids and I am running to join them. I see teacher blowing bubbles—red, yellow, green, blue. I see the bubbles up high and reach for them. I see some are moving down and so I wait to catch them!

When I catch a bubble, there is an explosion and it's gone. Where did it go?

I will get the next one!

THIS IS SO MUCH FUN!

ABOUT THE AUTHOR
Lisa M. Bennett O.D.

An optometrist who has been providing primary care eye exams for all ages for more than 20 years, Dr. Lisa M. Bennett has always been intrigued by the intersection of public health and eye care. Early in her career, Dr. Bennett noticed that children were not seen often in optometry offices for routine exams, despite the statistic that one in four children have a problem seeing. Since 1996, she has been involved in efforts to increase the number of children receiving full eye exams—the same exam that adults receive. *My Eyes and Me Growing to Three* is written to inform children, parents, teachers, health professionals and others of the importance of vision for children's development.

Dr. Bennett received her Bachelor of Arts from SUNY at Stony Brook University and her Doctorate from SUNY College of Optometry. Throughout her career she has been involved in various professional and community organizations such as National Optometric Association, American Optometric Association, American Academy of Orthokeratology and Myopia Control, Lions Club International, and the National Coalition of One Hundred Black Women.

ABOUT THE ILLUSTRATOR
Damien Dugger

Damien Dugger is an illustrator from Dinwiddie County, Virginia. Though he's been doing art for the majority of his life, entering art contests and taking advance art classes in school, he decided to take a step into illustration for children's books back in 2018. He welcomed the challenge that illustration presented. Using Procreate® on the Apple ipad to conduct his illustrations made the journey very helpful and now it's his go to for future projects.

Resources

The following information is provided in order to help learn about children's vision and eye health as well as locate a provider near you.

NATIONAL OPTOMETRIC ASSOCIATION

Website: nationaloptometricassociation.com/achieve

Email: mainoffice@natoptassoc.org

AMERICAN OPTOMETRIC ASSOCIATION

Website: aoa.org/healthy-eyes/health-for-life

text: 314.597.1939

INFANT SEE (a division of the AOA)

Website: infantsee.org

Email: infantsee@aoa.org

PREVENT BLINDNESS: NATIONAL CENTER FOR CHILDREN'S VISION AND EYE HEALTH.

Website: Nationalcenter.preventblindness.org

Email: info@preventblindness.org

LIONS CLUBS INTERNATIONAL

Lionsclubs.org

Lionsclubs.org/en/start-our-global-causes/vision

CPSIA information can be obtained
at www.ICGtesting.com
Printed in the USA
BVHW061230300922
648389BV00020B/768